W9-BKQ-620

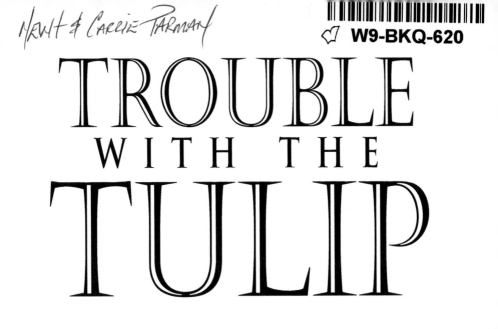

TROUBLE
WITH THE
TULIP

A Closer Examination of
The Five Points of Calvinism

FRANK S. PAGE, Ph.D.

RIVERSTONE GROUP
PUBLISHING

Design and Production
Riverstone Group, LLC, Canton, Georgia

Printed in Canada

TABLE OF
CONTENTS

INTRODUCTION

To say that the body of Christ is divided on many issues is perhaps the greatest understatement of the age. In fact, to use language that we all understand these days, the family of faith is *separated* because of seemingly irreconcilable differences. Some would say that a *divorce* has already occurred due to multiple issues. While the issues involved are too many to mention, they revolve not only around worship styles, practices, and choices, but around more weighty areas of theology and belief.

One of the most controversial issues in the body of Christ in these days is the issue of salvation. Specifically, the controversy revolves around how one believes that salvation is presented, secured and accepted. On one side of the issue there are those who are called *Calvinists*. Basically, these persons believe in a five point system of theology, developed by the reformer John Calvin and his followers. This system of theology has been called the "Biblical Theology of the Reformation," "Reformed Theology," or "Calvinism." The basic premise of this theology is that our Lord is the initiator, provider, and sole determining source regarding the salvation of human beings. He has chosen, according to His sovereign wisdom, those who are among the elect (who will be saved) and those who are the non-elect (those who will go to hell). This belief system holds to a belief in: Total depravity, Unconditional election, Limited atonement, Irresistible grace, and Perseverance of the saints.

Obviously, the first letters of each of the doctrinal beliefs form the acronym TULIP. This beautiful flower brings forth a wonderful picture in our minds, but the reality of the teachings of this system present a picture which is not quite so positive. Perhaps the words of Calvinist writer Curt Daniel portray it best. "All evangelical theologies will agree that salvation is solely by God's grace, but Calvinism alone says that it is sovereignly given to whomever God chooses to grant it." Then later he states, "There is a sense in which Christ died for all, but there is a sense in which He died only for the elect. We teach that the death of Christ is sufficient for all men, but is efficient only for the elect. He purchased some blessings for all men, but all blessings for some men."[1]

Writer R. B. Kuiper speaks a similar theme, "The universal and sincere offer of salvation does indeed presuppose the universal love of God, which is unmistakably taught in the scripture, but it does not presuppose that God purposed the salvation of all men by the death of His Son, which is nowhere taught in scripture."[2]

This "not so pretty" picture of our Lord is made even worse by the belief (on the part of some) that anyone who does not agree is totally out of touch with the wisdom of God. This kind of spirit is rampant and is illustrated by writer Loraine Boettner who said, "As will be shown, the Bible contains an abundance of material for the development of each of these doctrines. Furthermore, these are not isolated and independent doctrines but are so interrelated that they form a simple, harmonious, self-consistent system. Prove any one of them true and all the others will follow as logical and necessary parts of the system. Prove any one of them false, and the whole system must be abandoned."[3]

I want to very clearly state that my intention in this book is not simply to disprove the philosophical system of Calvinism, though I believe that will occur. Instead of adhering to a system of logic, which many seek to do or adhering in blind devotion to the teachings of any one scholar, as some are prone to do, I propose that we look to God's Word for His clear teaching. Many books on Calvinism begin with a harsh denunciation of the doctrine of Arminianism (which I will explain later). Similarly, other books begin with an intense denunciation of Calvinism. It is my belief that there is a precious teaching in God's Word which will lead us to the truth about God's salvation.

I do believe in predestination, election, and foreknowledge, but I still have trouble with the TULIP!

I do want to state at the beginning that I do believe in predestination, election, and foreknowledge (words which will be defined later) but I still have trouble with the TULIP! In this work, I shall attempt to help the reader see that the terms just mentioned are biblical terms and are a part of a beautiful story, a biblical story of salvation. They form a portion of the story of God's gift of grace to His people, a grace that is both a saving grace and an enabling grace.

This book will attempt to relate to any person who is struggling to understand this seemingly complex and controversial area. While every attempt has been made to thoroughly study the scholars who have written great works, the historians who have long pondered these questions, as well as the appropriate scriptures, my hope is that this book will be a valuable aid to God's church people to use in understanding God's great yet simple salvation. As a theologian who is also a pastor, I have a deep yearning for God's people to be thoroughly equipped.

I shall attempt to help you understand the history behind the controversy. I will attempt to describe the basic positions which are held by most people throughout the Christian family. We will discuss Calvinism, Arminianism and related positions. I will also deal with some issues which I feel are deeply important if we are to understand a Scripturally based soteriology (study of salvation). It is my belief that the issue which is before us has direct implications regarding the nature of God, the issue of freedom, as well as the issue of God's plan for us. Then, we shall attempt to provide a Scriptural definition to the key words which are often used in this controversy. As we do so, we will also attempt to study the key passages of scripture which are most often used.

Our God is an awesome God and it is true that He

works in mysterious ways. However, I do believe that His Word gives us a very clear direction regarding His plan for our lives. One Calvinist writer, William Shed said, "The doctrine of predestination is too hard for new Christians. Never teach it to babies in Christ. Predestination is for the settled, mature Christians only."[4] I do not agree at all! I believe that God's Word should be taught to all of His people. I ask that you would read this book with your Bible open, your mind ready to receive, and your heart open to the Holy Spirit's guidance.

A BRIEF HISTORY

The New Testament church taught that Jesus Christ died for all people. It was their belief that salvation occurred by receiving God's unmerited favor (grace) through faith (Ephesians 2:8). A perfect example of an expression of this is found in Acts 2:37-41. The Apostle Peter had been boldly proclaiming the truth about Jesus Christ. The scriptures clearly show that those who heard this were pierced to the heart and asked, "What shall we do?" At this point, Peter did *not* tell them that there was nothing that they could do, for salvation was simply a sovereign act of a sovereign God! Instead of stating that philosophical belief, he stated the truth that they were to "Repent . . . " He finished his exhortation by saying, "Save yourselves from this corrupt generation." The results are found in v. 41 where the scripture says, "Those who accepted his message were baptized."

The New Testament church taught that Jesus Christ died for all people.

It is quite obvious in the early church that there was a belief that salvation was a precious gift from God, yet that gift could be received through faith by those who were pierced to the heart. There is no doubt that the Holy Spirit which had been promised by Jesus and given at Pentecost was the convicting power by which God drew these lost persons into a recognition of their need to repent and believe. The scripture is clear that the Holy Spirit is the agent of conviction (John 16:8). It is God the Holy Spirit who draws men and women to Christ.

There was no question in the hearts of the New Testament church as to the God-given ability of all persons to respond to God's invitation. As a result, the early church grew at a phenomenal numerical rate.

The apostolic fathers, such as Barnabas, Clement and Ignatius, etc. continued to believe and teach the same New Testament doctrine mentioned earlier. They continued to teach a belief that salvation was a God-given gift but one which could be received or rejected.[5]

As the decades turned into centuries, the church of Jesus Christ began to develop different thought systems or theologies about various issues. Contrary to what some denominations might say, the early church was not tightly organized around doctrinal or denominational lines. However, normally there was a sufficient unity of understanding about basic Christian doctrines. Those who differed from those basic, orthodox understandings were often brought to trial in church-type judicial settings called councils. Some of the great councils were as follows:

1. The Council of Nicaea (A.D. 325). This Council sought to judge between the merits of a leader

named Arius who sought to provide understanding regarding the mystery of Christ's human and divine natures. About 318 A.D. Arius decided that it would compromise the dignity and honor of God the Father to say that Jesus Christ was of the same divine, eternal essence as God. Consequently, he worked out a system which declared that Christ was a being who had been created before time and though greater than man was less than God. A young deacon from the church in Alexandria named Athanasius became the champion of the orthodox view which stated that Jesus Christ was indeed coequal with God the Father.

2. The First Council of Constantinople (A.D. 381). In this series of meetings, Apollinarius' views were condemned because he denied the true manhood (humanity) of Christ.

3. The Council of Ephesus (A.D. 431). In this trial, Nestorius was declared guilty of heresy. Bishops Cyril and Celestine condemned the Nestorians, followers of Nestorius, feeling that their teachings disrupted the unity of Christ's person and so separated Christ's nature into human and divine as to deny the deity of Christ. By the way, one of Nestorius' greatest objections was to calling the Virgin Mary, "theotokos," or the mother of God. He asserted that Mary might be called the mother of Jesus' human nature but certainly should not be viewed as the mother of Christ's divine nature, as the term might suggest.

4. The Council of Chalcedon (A.D. 451). In this controversy, Eutychus took the position that after the
incarnation Christ had only one nature and that it
was divine. The Council affirmed the clear distinc-
tion between Christ's human and divine nature and
stated that Christ is one person in two natures.

It is important to note that during the Council of
Ephesus in A.D. 431, there was another very important
discussion. Another group was also condemned, namely
the Pelagians. Pelagius was a British monk who had fled
from Britain to Italy and then later to North Africa about
A.D. 411. He taught that it was not necessary that a child
be baptized, since he had no original sin to be washed
away. Such a direct denial of one of the major beliefs of
the early church brought prompt bickering. The Pelagians
believed that every person could choose to sin or choose
to be righteous. At the Council in 431 at Ephesus, the
Pelagian view was officially condemned, along with the
Nestorians with whom the Pelagians had been friendly.[6]

To truly understand this argument, one needs to be
familiar with the teachings of Augustine. Augustine was a
great theologian of the fourth and fifth centuries. In his
book, Confessions, he explains his doctrines in great detail.
In response to the Pelagian controversy, Augustine asserted that Adam had been created with freedom, but that in
Adam's fall all mankind had lost its purity and freedom.
Thus, Augustine believed that babies needed to be baptized to wash away the guilt of this original sin. He also
taught that the sacraments of the Catholic church were
necessary to preserve the individual from additional guilt.

In regard to salvation, he insisted that persons could not work for salvation, that even the ability to accept salvation is a gift of God. This led to his belief that God chooses those who should be saved and enables them to be saved. Robert Baker rightly points out the inconsistency of Augustine's theology. "In his emphasis upon God's sovereignty, Augustine left nothing for man to do in salvation; yet he demanded that infants be baptized in order to be saved from inherited guilt. If God predestined a child to be saved, it would appear that baptism would have little effect in attempting to accomplish the same thing."[7]

Over the years, the universal church continued to split into various factions and belief systems. The Reformation was perhaps the most major split. The division between the Roman Catholic church and the Protestants revolved around the issues of the church and its teaching regarding salvation. Roman Catholic theology held that the Roman Catholic church was the only true church and that salvation could only be experienced through an adherence to the sacraments of the church. Protestants believed that persons come to the Lord through belief in Christ. Martin Luther's personal discovery of Christ through the teachings of Romans 5 provided a foundation for this belief. The revelation in his heart that we are "justified by faith" (Romans 5:1) set him free from the belief that he had to work for his salvation.

As time went on, the protestant group quickly became protestant groups. Various interpretations of scripture and adherence to differing beliefs and polity led to the development of denominationalism as is seen today. At times these groups sought to develop new doctrines, while others chose to modify or to continue the existing doctrines or practices of the Catholic church. For example, some held to the Augustinian teachings regarding salvation, while others broke from this and declared their belief on a more scriptural foundation.

One of the Reformation leaders and writers whose thoughts became very influential was John Calvin. Calvin was born in France in 1509. In 1536, he published the first edition of his signature work, *The Institutes of the Christian Religion.* Through the growing influence of his writings and a strong support system of friends, he eventually was able to change the city of Geneva, Switzerland into a city government based on his theological teachings. In his teachings and their subsequent enforcement by civil authorities, he strongly taught the doctrine of predestination. While this will be discussed later, he taught that God had predestined some to be elect (saved) and others to be non-elect (lost). His teaching of this Augustinian belief also led him to continue an emphasis upon infant baptism.

Calvin switched absolutes! Calvin's insistence upon the absolute sovereignty of God substituted this belief for the biblical view of salvation by grace through faith!

While some accurately point out Calvin's rejection of sacramental salvation (taught by Augustine), we need to understand that Calvin switched absolutes! Whereas Augustine had developed an absolute system of belief in the church's power to save through the sacraments,

Calvin's insistence upon the absolute sovereignty of God substituted this belief for the biblical view of salvation by grace through faith!

This system of belief was refuted by many. It led to a serious number of questions. For example, are we saved by grace or by faith? Calvin's answer to this question was to arbitrarily make faith subservient to grace: God gives elect men a special kind of faith for salvation. In this way predestination was given priority over every other doctrine and became the controlling principle of Reformation theology.[8] Author Mildred Bangs Wynkoop makes the strong yet accurate statement, "The theory of personal predestination was not, then derived from biblical exegesis but from a doctrine demanded by logical necessity to defend the absolute sovereignty of God against the sovereignty of the church.[9] One of the major opponents to Calvin's philosophy was a Dutch theologian named Jacob Hermann who is best known by the Latin form of his last name, Arminius. Arminius had serious doubts about the sovereign grace as it was preached by other reformers, such as Calvin. His followers developed his doctrine further and finally formulated them into what is called "Five Points of Arminianism." These doctrines will be discussed later. These Arminian followers were determined to present their belief system to the officials for their consideration. In 1618, a national conference was convened in Dort to examine these teachings. Many Calvinist writers love to point out that this seven month long conference ended in the declaration that Arminianism was heretical. It is also important to note that it was during this conference, called the Synod of Dort, that the five points of Calvinism were formulated in order to counter the Arminianism system.

The truth about the Synod of Dort is that 102 Dutch orthodox Calvinists were official members of this conference, together with 28 foreign delegates. Only 13 Arminian representatives were present but because they were prisoners of the state due to their treasonist views about theology, they had no vote. This well known historical fact is for some reason totally absent from most books extolling the virtues of Calvinism which emanate from the Synod of Dort!

Needless to say, Calvin's system became a part of orthodox Christianity's statement of faith. It was incorporated into what is called the Westminster Confession of Faith. Deviation from it of course has occurred, but only under strenuous objections. John Calvin said himself, "The subject of predestination, which in itself is contended with considerable difficulty, is rendered very perplexed, and hence perilous by human curiosity, which cannot be restrained from wandering into forbidden paths and climbing into the clouds, determined if it can that none of the secret things of God shall remain unexplored."[10] Calvin's prophecy was indeed true. Human curiosity can indeed be a frivolous thing, but it is often encouraged by the Holy Spirit's teaching ministry. Since the teachings of Calvin and their inclusion into orthodox statements of faith, multitudes of believers have sought a biblical understanding of salvation rather than accepting either Calvinism or Arminianism.

Later, John Wesley encountered the writings of Arminius and was deeply impressed by them. In fact, he edited a magazine for many years called *The Arminian*, in which holiness doctrine was proclaimed. Perhaps Wesley's greatest divergence with Calvin was in the issue of the image of God. To Wesley and those who followed in his belief system, the image of God is marred in every part, but not destroyed, because to destroy that image would deprive men of humanhood. In other words, the only reason any semblance of humanhood is preserved is by the free grace of God. Without grace, men would bear the image of the devil.[11]

Many love to point out that even later in history, Charles Hadden Spurgeon, the great preacher of England, was an ardent Calvinist. While it is true that Spurgeon was indeed a strong believer in the sovereign grace and salvation of God, it also needs to be pointed out that he had serious opposition to both the belief and practice of "hyper-Calvinism." While this extreme, five point Calvinism will be discussed later, let it be known that Spurgeon was quoted as saying, "Hyper-Calvinism not only causes personal lop-sidedness, but what is more serious, it

Spurgeon was often criticized by the hyper-Calvinists.

prevents a full preaching of the gospel."[12] Spurgeon was often criticized by the hyper-Calvinists because of his preaching of the gospel to large audiences, without regard to the fact that non-elect persons might be present. In response to this, Spurgeon said, "They dare not come out and preach as Peter did, 'Repent ye, and be converted that your sins may be blotted out.'" It must also be admitted that Spurgeon repeatedly opposed Arminianism. With the total agreement of this writer, he particularly objected to the belief of the possibility of a final fall from grace and called it "the wickedest falsehood on earth."[13] Spurgeon did believe that there is a common call always given to men to come to Christ. However he believed that "all of them that love God love Him because they have had a special irresistible, supernatural call.[14]

As one might imagine, there have been many throughout the last centuries who have adhered to both Calvinism, Arminianism, or a belief system with elements of both. In 1814, the Baptists of the United States divided over the issue of evangelism and missions. The anti-missionary groups (hyper-Calvinists) have dwindled almost to the vanishing point. The group committed to evangelism and missions has flourished. Southern Baptists, the most committed, are the largest non-Catholic religious body in the nation.[15] However, in recent days there has been a resurgence among some in evangelical, even Baptist circles who hold to this doctrine.

A DESCRIPTION OF POSITIONS

As stated earlier, there have been a variety of variations of thought which have developed over the years in regards to Calvinism, Arminianism, etc. Following is an attempt to describe the basic positions according to the most often used definitions.

THE FIVE POINTS OF CALVINISM - TULIP

Total Depravity

Calvin believed that in the Garden of Eden, when Adam and Eve fell into sin, the image of God in human beings was totally destroyed, making man wholly and irrevocably corrupt in this life and incapable of any act or word or thought untainted by that corruption. Most would say that sin has gone so deep into human nature that it cannot be eradicated. Grace covers sin but cannot cure it. Dwayne Spencer states it this way, "Unregenerate man is in absolute bondage to Satan, and wholly incapable of exercising his own will freely to trust in Christ."[16]

Other Calvinist writers point out that when they speak of total depravity, they do not mean that every man is as evil as he might possibly be. They do not mean that people are unable to do any good toward their fellow man or even to give outward allegiance toward God. Seaton states, "The whole personality of man has been affected by the fall, and sin extends to the whole of the faculties–the will, the understanding, the affections, and all else."[17]

Some of the scriptures used to affirm this understanding are Genesis 6:5, Jeremiah 17:9, Romans 3:10-11, Ephesians 2:2-3, I Corinthians 2:14.

Unconditional Election

This doctrine is at the very heart of the Calvinists' understanding of salvation. Simply put, this belief means that God has unconditionally chosen some to be saved and some to be lost. Humans, because of their depravity, can do nothing to merit salvation. Personal volition or faith has nothing to do with it. Only God's unconditional choice is at work. John 15:6 is used, for example, to show that the choice has to do with God's perspective and not mankind's. In his book Spencer says, "It is tantamount to blasphemy for anyone to argue that man is capable, of his own free will, to make a decision for Christ."[18] Daniel states this belief clearly when he says, "All evangelical theologies will agree that salvation is solely by God's grace, but Calvinism alone says that it is sovereignly given to whomever God chooses to grant it."[19]

Many scriptures are used to defend this belief. Some of them are Romans 8:28-29, Romans 9:11, I Corinthians 1:26-29, I Timothy 1:9, John 15:16, Ephesians 1:4, Acts 13:48, and John 6:37.

When Calvinists are asked to explain the rationale

behind God's unconditional election, some warn not to even attempt such an understanding. Even Calvin himself stated such questioning centers around the "'foolishness' of mere men attempting to 'penetrate the inner recesses of divine wisdom.'"[20] Others say that God not only chose some humans for salvation and others for damnation, but He also chose nations for His purpose while ignoring others. Seaton states, "Why should God choose the nation of Israel as His peculiar people? There is no need to speculate, for Deuteronomy 7:7 gives the answer: 'The Lord did not set His love upon you, nor choose you, because you were more in number than any people; for you are the fewest of all people; but because the Lord loved you . . . '"[21] Others are more bold in their explanation of God's reasoning. Loraine Boettner states, "The condemnation of the non-elect is designed primarily to furnish external exhibition, before men and angels, of God's hatred for sin."[22] He also states that, "The reason that God did not choose all to eternal life was not because He did not wish to save all, but that for reasons we cannot fully explain a universal choice would have been inconsistent with His perfect righteousness."[23] Perhaps the most interesting of his comments deal with the issue of Satan's role. He states, "Even the works of Satan are so controlled and limited that they serve God's purposes. While Satan eagerly desires the destruction of the wicked and diligently works to bring it about, yet the destruction proceeds from God. It is in the first place, God who decrees that the wicked shall suffer and Satan is merely permitted to lay the punishment upon them."[24]

Some venture to say that it is God's foreknowledge that is the impetus behind His predestination. In other words, since God knows who is going to be saved, He predestines those persons according to His plan. Seaton disagrees with this and says, "It will not do to say that God elected us because He saw something that we would do, that is accept His Son. We are not chosen because we perform such a holy work as accepting Christ, but we are chosen so that we might be able to accept Him."[25] This belief is held by many Calvinist writers, who basically say that election is not because of believing, but believing is on account of our being elected or ordained to eternal life.

Limited Atonement

This teaching states that if one believes that the Bible teaches that God is sovereign, that His plan is unchangeable, and that His election is unconditional, one must conclude that the atonement of Jesus Christ is limited to those whom He willed to make the objects of His grace. Spencer states the Calvinist line quite clearly, "Christ did not die for all men. Atonement was limited! Redemption was particular! Only the elect bride of Christ was the object of His love."[26] While several scriptures are used to defend this belief (such as Romans 8:31-33, Ephesians 5:25, Ephesians 1:4, Galatians 1:3-5, John 10:14-15, I Peter 2:9, etc.), much time is spent explaining away the passages which portray a universal application for the atonement.

One writer states, "There is the sense in which Christ died for all, but there is a sense in which He died only for the elect. We teach that the death of Christ is sufficient for all men, but is efficient only for the elect. He purchased some blessings for all men, but all blessings for some men."[27] Others say things such as, "In some of the passages which teach that the atonement was for 'all,' for 'the world,' or for 'every man,' the meaning of these verses is restricted by the context."[28] Shed states it this way, "The scripture which says 'whosoever will' or 'all who believe' really means those to whom faith is given."[29]

Irresistible Grace

This means that God's all-powerful nature and sole responsibility in salvation implies that His grace cannot be resisted. Calvinistic writers see this as absolutely logical. If God is the determiner of salvation and the sole agent by which it is accomplished, then a human being cannot be involved in any shape, form, or fashion in its implementation or acceptance. Thus it is only logical that they would be irresistibly drawn to the Lord. Passages which are often used to defend this belief are John 6:37, 44, 45, Romans 8:14, Revelation 1:15, I Peter 2:9, and I Peter 2:10. One writer states, "When the Holy Spirit calls a man, or a woman, or a young person by His grace, that call is irresistible: it cannot be frustrated; it is a manifestation of God's irresistible grace."[30] God's power in sovereignty in regards to other areas of life is stated by one writer in this way, "God so governs the inward feelings, external environment, habits, desires, motives, etc., of men that they freely do what He purposes. This operation is inscrutable, but nonetheless real."[31]

Perseverance of the Saints

This belief states that God's children can never be lost since their salvation is by the will of the unchanging, omnipotent, sovereign God. Scriptures which are used to defend this belief are Romans 8:28-39, Romans 8:27, Philippians 1:6, John 6:39, etc.

This belief teaches that since no condition in man determines his being chosen or elect (because scripture teaches unconditional election), it stands to reason there is nothing he can do to remove himself from grace. If perseverance depends upon a person who has a fallen sin nature, he would be totally without hope.

FIVE POINTS OF ARMINIANISM

In 1618, several persons who disagreed with the stated orthodox faith of the state church, led by John Calvin, presented their beliefs to the Dutch parliament. These beliefs became known as the five points of Arminianism.

Free Will

As one can see, this issue was at the heart of the disagreement. Arminius or as he was actually known, Jacob Hermann, had objected to Calvin's continued adherence to Augustine's belief in the sovereignty of God to the exclusion of human free will. This position normally held to the belief that the fall of man was not as total as the Calvinists and the Catholics taught. Human beings could certainly choose good or evil. Even though we are all influenced by sin, the Arminians believed that there was still enough good left in mankind for him/her to accept Christ for salvation.

Conditional Election

Conditional election taught that election was based

upon the foreknowledge of God as to who would believe. A person's act of faith was the "condition" for their being elected to eternal life, since God foresaw this person exercising their "free will" positively toward Jesus Christ. In other words, a person created his own condition through faith, but since God's all-knowing nature foresaw that occurrence, that foreknowledge is what is meant by predestination. Ephesians 1:5 is one such instance in which this predestination is described.

Universal Atonement

Arminians taught and believed that Christ died for all. Scriptures such as John 3:16 and II Corinthians 5:14-15 are used among a multitude of scriptures which teach this truth. This teaching insists that atonement is universal. Christ died for everyone and offers the gift freely. Every individual must choose to accept or reject that gift.

Obstructable or Resistible Grace

Arminians taught that since God wanted all of mankind to be saved, He sent the Holy Spirit to draw all men to Christ. The human will, however, is free to reject the drawing power of the Holy Spirit. An example of scriptural defense of this would be found in Matthew 13 where Jesus teaches the parable of the sower and the soils. Obviously some reject the good seed before it even takes hold. Others allow it to be stolen through other personal decisions.

Falling from Grace

The last point of Arminianism is the teaching that a person can also "will" himself or herself to be lost. Since salvation can be received, it can also be rejected after it has been received. Some may use Luke 8:13 (again, the parable of the soils) to talk about the ability to fall away. Others use scriptures, such as Hebrews 6:6, which speak about the possibility of falling away.

FIVE POINTS OF SCRIPTURAL SOTERIOLOGY (THEOLOGY OF SALVATION)

Rather than accepting a belief system which is based upon a reformer's beliefs or teachings, I propose that we adopt God's teaching on salvation. It is time for the clear communication of a biblically based understanding of how God has reached out to sinful humanity and how sinful humanity can come into God's kingdom. In other words, it is time for a clear understanding of the doctrine of grace! Perhaps the greatest, single place in which this grace is described is Titus 2:11-14. It begins with the beautiful statement, "For the grace of God that brings salvation has appeared to all men." Then the passage goes on to portray the beautiful teaching ministry of grace which is not only a saving grace but is also an enabling grace.

For a way to remember this description of salvation, let us use the word grace as an acrostic.

G - Given through Christ (election)

R - Rejected through rebellion (resistible grace)

A - Accepted through faith (freedom of will)

C - Christ died for all (unlimited atonement)

E - Everlasting life = security of the believer (perseverance of the Saints)

G - Grace Given Through Christ

Literally hundreds of scriptures refer to God's grace (His unmerited favor) which He chose to provide through Christ. One of the most precious is John 10:10 in which Jesus affirms that "I have come that you might have life." Later, Jesus said it clearly in John 5:24 when He said, "I tell you the truth, whoever hears my word and believes Him who sent me has eternal life and will not be condemned; he has crossed over from death to life."

The beautiful truth is that God's grace is God's means of election.

The beautiful truth is that God's grace is God's means of election! In other words, God's election of believers is because of His grace and directly based in His grace. That truth is expressed in Ephesians 1-2. In essence, Paul states in these two chapters that God elected a way of salvation as well as a people to propagate that way. In Ephesians 1:4 we find the words, "He chose us." This translates the Greek word which was later anglicized as elected. Please note that Paul says that God chose us or elected us "in Him" or in Christ. Second Corinthians 5:19 picks up on this thought beautifully, "God was reconciling the world to Himself in Christ, not counting men's sins against them." Please note that he was not referring to a limited few, but to the whole world. In eleven verses (Ephesians 1:3-13), Paul uses "in Christ" or its equivalent eleven times.[32]

Ephesians 1:5 again states His precious gift. He provided this wonderful grace so that we might be adopted as His sons, through Jesus Christ. It was done "in accordance with His pleasure and will." This does indeed express God's sovereignty. This means that God acts in accord with His nature and purpose by redeeming mankind through the electing force of Jesus' love, mercy, and unmerited favor.

R - Grace May Be Rejected Through Rebellion

The issue of the freedom of the will is of paramount importance. Human beings do have the ability to choose. If it were all a predetermined proposition ahead of time, why did Jesus weep (in Luke 19:41) over Jerusalem? Why did He not simply state that it was His Father's intention for the city to be destroyed along with the non-elect? In John 5:40, when Jesus agonized over His rejection, why did He state that "you refused to come to Me to have life"? Did He not realize, according to Calvinists, that people cannot refuse to come to Christ? Did He not know that if people are non-elect, they cannot reject, for they cannot decide?

In John 5:40, when Jesus agonized over His rejection, why did He state that "you refused to come to Me to have life"? Did He not realize, according to Calvinists, that people cannot refuse to come to Christ? Did He not know that if people are non-elect, they cannot reject, for they cannot decide?

God's wonderful grace can be rejected through rebellion. Here we do find some agreement with Calvinists (in regards to the issue of total depravity). All true believers know that according to Romans 3:23, "All have sinned, and fall short of the glory of God." There should be general agreement in what Isaiah 64:6 says, "All our righteous acts are like filthy rags." It is true that, "we all, like sheep, have gone astray, each of us has turned to his own way" (Isaiah 53:6).

There was great debate at this point between Calvin's followers and John Wesley's followers. In Calvinism, the image of God was thought to be totally destroyed during the fall making men wholly and irrevocably corrupt in this life. According to Wesley and others who follow in his thought, the image of God is marred in every part but not destroyed, because to destroy the image would deprive men of humanity. In Wesley's view, the only reason any semblance of humanity is preserved is by the free grace of God. Without grace, men would bear the image of the devil[33] One may discuss these fine points 'til Jesus returns!

However, I call again for a scriptural understanding. The scripture does indeed provide a clear picture of humanity that is affected in every part by sin. After all that is the reason Christ came to suffer and die. Romans 5:8 says it well, "But God demonstrates his own love for us in this: While we were still sinners, Christ died for us."

W. T. Conner said it well, "Persons are free beings with the power of self-determination. They can be influenced but not forced. They have the capacity for choice. They do what they will to do. Their freedom is limited but real. They have the power to establish ideals and plans and to move toward those ideals."[34] Part of that ability to choose is to choose the way of rebellion against the Lord. Jesus predicted that most would choose that way when He said in Matthew 7:13-14, "For wide is the gate and broad is the road that leads to destruction, and many enter through it. But small is the gate and narrow the road that leads to life, and only a few find it."

We must also recognize that those who do perish by the rejection of Christ's atoning death do so because they resisted, not because of God's rejection of their election. Several scriptural examples point to the tragedy of this rejection. In Luke 7:30, the Pharisees "rejected God's purpose for themselves." In Stephen's great sermon in Acts 7, he pointed out their rejection by saying, "You always resist the Holy Spirit!" (v. 51). Similarly, Paul and Barnabas pointed out the rejection of those in Antioch in Acts 13:46 when they said, "Since you reject it and do not consider yourselves worthy of eternal life, we now turn to the Gentiles."

Roy Fish of Southwestern Seminary accurately points out that Calvinists believe that because of the total depravity of mankind, they can't respond to God in repentance and faith. In other words, "Dead people can't respond." Fish quickly reminds us that Adam and Eve sinned against God and became spiritually dead. Yet, when God spoke to them in the garden, they heard Him. People who are dead in trespasses and sins can hear the voice of God.[35]

A - Grace Can Be Accepted Through Faith

Just as human beings have the freedom to reject God's call through rebellion, they also have the glorious opportunity to accept it through faith. The great passage so often discussed in Ephesians 2 contains the great truth of mankind's ability to accept God's gift through faith. In Ephesians 2:8 it clearly says, "For it is by grace you have been saved, through faith." Virtually every sermon recorded in the New Testament is a sermon which calls for mankind's acceptance of the truth. Over and over, in great emotional appeal, the apostles called out for their listeners to hear and to respond. Peter called out in Acts 3:19, "Repent, then, and turn to God, so that your sins may be wiped out, that times of refreshing may come from the Lord." According to Calvinism, man's will is moved by grace prior to man's consciousness of it and apart from his awareness of it. A scriptural view recognizes just what Acts 3:19 teaches. One must turn to God before one's sins may be wiped out.

God's great desire is that everyone might accept Him! Second Peter 3:9 is abundantly clear at this point, "He is patient with you, not wanting anyone to perish, but everyone to come to repentance." When true repentance takes place in a life, it is accompanied by saving faith in Jesus Christ. Conversely, when a person believes in Christ with genuine, saving faith, repentance from sin is present. It is important to note that many are teaching false doctrine at this point. Some teach a backward view of salvation. One Calvinistic writer says, "A man is not saved because he believes in Christ; he believes in Christ because he is saved."[36] However, the scripture says, "Believe in the Lord Jesus and you will be saved" (Acts 16:31). The offer has been made to all, but may be rejected through rebellion or accepted through faith.

C - Grace Means That Christ Died for All

Again, look to the great passage found in Titus 2:11. In non-equivocal terms, Paul states that the grace that brings salvation "appeared to all." Paul does not mention a select group nor a preferred few. He presents a biblical view of salvation which shows an unlimited atonement. It needs to be mentioned that some have taken these verses out of context over the years to promote a universal salvation (that all will be saved). The Bible nowhere teaches a universal salvation! Jesus' teaching in Matthew 25:46 teaches that some "will go away to eternal punishment but the righteous to eternal life."

Even though the scriptures do not teach universal salvation, they do indeed teach the unlimited atonement of Christ.

Even though the scriptures do not teach universal salvation, they do teach the unlimited atonement of Christ. Not only does God desire all people to be saved (I Timothy 2:4, Luke 13:34, John 3:16-17, etc.) but also that Christ died for all mankind. A great example of this desire is found in Matthew 18:14, "In the same way your Father in heaven is not willing that any of these little ones should be lost." Other passages which are supportive of this truth are Luke 19:10, John 3:16, II Corinthians 5:14-15, I Timothy 2:4, I John 2:2, I John 4:4 and Hebrews 2:9.

E - Grace Insures Everlasting Life

This teaching is sometimes called the eternal security of the believer as well as perseverance of the saints. The scriptures clearly teach that true believers will never fall away from the state of grace, but will persevere. Please note that it is true believers, not superficial ones, who will persevere. Matthew 7:21 is a pertinent scripture which teaches that many will call God their Lord, but will not be in heaven. Only those who have a relationship and commitment to the Lord will be in heaven. However, those who have truly been saved will be eternally saved. Some use passages such as Hebrews 5:11-6:12 to talk about the possibility of falling from grace. In reality, the author is saying that it cannot happen! In the hypothetical case that it could happen, the author says that those who had turned their backs on Christ could never again accept Him, for that would be crucifying Christ all over.

The scripture is very clear at this point. Passages such as John 3:16 talk about everlasting life, not life until one sins to a certain degree. John 10:27-28 states the truth of the eternal security of the believer by pointing out that, "My sheep listen to my voice; I know them, and they follow me. I give them eternal life, and they shall never perish; no one can snatch them out of my hand." John 5:24 says it well also, "I tell you the truth, whoever hears my word and believes him who sent me has eternal life and will not be condemned; he has crossed over from death to life." Romans 8:35-39 enumerates the many things which

Birth is an irrevocable experience. It places one into a family. Spiritually, when one is born again, they are born into the family of God which is eternal.

might be able to separate us from the love of God. Paul

indicates that none of these can do so. Saving faith is eternal faith! The teachings of the Lord in John 3 point out the necessity to be born again. As everyone knows, when one is born physically, it cannot be undone. Similarly, when one is born again spiritually, it cannot be undone. Birth is an irrevocable experience. It places one into a family. Spiritually, when one is born again, they are born into the family of God which is eternal.

FIVE POINTS OF CALVINISM	FIVE POINTS OF ARMINIANISM	FIVE POINTS OF SCRIPTURAL SOTERIOLOGY (The Theology of Salvation)
Total Depravity	Free Will	G - Given Through Christ
Unconditional Election	Conditional Election	R - Rejected Through Rebellion
Limited Atonement	Universal Atonement	A - Accepted Through Faith
Irresistible Grace	Obstructable or Resistible Grace	C - Christ Died for All
Perseverance of the Saints	Falling from Grace	E - Everlasting Life = Security of the Believer

THE CALL FOR A SCRIPTURALLY-BASED UNDERSTANDING OF SALVATION

Even taking into account the few scriptures which on the surface may seem to support Calvinistic or Arminian doctrine, they are overwhelmed by the massive number of simple, obvious scriptures which teach the true nature of God's salvation. As you may have already gathered, I do have points of agreement with both Calvinistic and Arminian doctrine. For example, we agree that the new birth may be explained as a transaction that can be accomplished only by our Lord. While a human being may accept or reject God's gift, the gift is paid for, presented by and given by the Lord Himself. We also agree that lost human beings are spiritually dead. They are incapable of worshiping God. They are in darkness and are blinded by the god of this age (Satan himself). God uses the work of the Holy Spirit, the Word of God and the witness of the believer to draw sinners unto Himself. John 6:44-45 says it well, "No one can come to me unless the Father who sent me draws him, and I will raise him up at the last day. It is written in the Prophets: 'They will all be taught by God.' Everyone who listens to the Father and learns from him comes to me." A biblically-based concept of salvation must contain an understanding of the majestic work of God, including His drawing Holy Spirit but also free acceptance. God did not wish for His creation to be robots who accept His way without thought, emotion, and passion. A biblically-based understanding of salvation includes all the above elements.

THE NATURE OF GOD

One of the most neglected areas of discussion in the debate between Calvinism, Arminianism and those who would seek a more biblical base for understanding is the study of the nature of God. At the very heart of this argument is the question, "What kind of God do we serve?" Is Yahweh God a God of love? First John 4:8 says that He is! Even given the interpretive gymnastics which some writers use to explain away God's love, all must accept that John 3:16 expresses His love profoundly. There are some who have so profoundly accepted the teachings of others, such as John Calvin, that they have pushed aside God's love for an emphasis upon God's sovereignty. In so doing, many have presented a picture of a God whose nature is cruel and unloving. While the issue of God's sovereignty is important and deserving of careful consideration, one must be careful not to overemphasize its place. Yes, the word is found five times in the New Testament (NIV), but if one is not careful, then an overemphasis on sovereignty issues can lead to a distorted concept in which God is responsible for everything. As we will see later in a description of certain often used phrases, some have come to the point where God is credited and blamed for everything. Some Calvinists even believe that Satan's work in the destruction of the lost is simply a part of God's eternal plan.

The Bible says in Ephesians 4-5 "in love He predestined us." Therefore we need to remember that whatever God did, He did it in love.

Rather than a God who is cold and cruel, the scripture tells of a God who lovingly cares for His creation just as a "hen gathers her chicks under her wings" (Luke 13:34) or a good shepherd that lays down his life for his sheep (John 10:11). Can you imagine Jesus, God's Son, saying, "Come to me all you who are weary and burdened and I will give you rest, unless you are of the non-elect, then get away from me!" No, in Matthew 11:28-30 He said, "Come to me, *all* you who are weary and burdened, and I will give you rest. Take my yoke upon you and learn from me, for I am gentle and humble in heart, and you will find rest for your souls. For my yoke is easy and my burden is light."

Rather than a God who is cold and cruel, the scripture teaches of a God who lovingly cares for His creation.

The true nature of God is not shown by a Calvinistic theology that presents a God who selects one to be saved and another to be lost. On the contrary, the true nature of God is portrayed through scripture such as the parable of the lost sheep. In Matthew 18, can you imagine if Jesus had said, "In the same way your Father in heaven is willing that some of these little ones should be lost"? Instead He said, "In the same way your Father in heaven is not willing that any of these little ones should be lost." Calvinism teaches that our God selects some children to be saved and some to be condemned! That teaching portrays a God with whom I am unfamiliar!

There are many persons belonging to churches that officially believe "five point" Calvinism. Many of them express surprise when they are told what their church truly believes. I would like to challenge all who truly believe in five point Calvinism to *stop being closet Calvinists!* If you truly believe these doctrines, then let others know about it. They need to know what you believe.

In Matthew 18, can you imagine if Jesus had said, "In the same way your Father in heaven is willing that some of these little ones should be lost"?

THE ISSUE OF FREEDOM

In a tirade against freedom of will, one author said, "It is a perverted and dishonoring view of God to imagine Him struggling along with disobedient men, doing the best He can to convert them, but not able to accomplish His purpose."[37] On the contrary, the Bible pictures a God who does just that! He struggles to do everything He can to reach the hearts of lost men and women. Even as they cruelly lashed out at Jesus on the cross, He was able to respond back with a plea to the Father in Luke 23:34 and say, "Father, forgive them, for they do not know what they're doing." We serve a God who loves immensely, but does not force His love upon us. He gives freedom of choice.

The issue of free will is at the very heart of this matter. From the very beginning, we see this important element. In the Garden of Eden, God did not create Adam and Eve as individuals who were predestined to serve Him out of blind obedience or robotic action. Free will was an essential part of His plan, if people were to choose to love Him. He did not want creatures who would follow blindly out of duty. He wanted children who would love Him and accept Him and receive His great gift of grace. His continued call for willing love is seen as He dealt with the people of Israel in Deuteronomy 30. In vs. 19-20 He said, "Now choose life, so that you and your children may live and that you may love the Lord your God, listen to his voice, and hold fast to him." Again, the issue is freedom of the will. He gave them the ability to choose and urged them to do so. Our Lord Jesus knew that most would not choose to receive His grace. In Matthew 7:13-14, He does indeed say that most will follow the road that leads to destruction and few the road that leads to life.

I agree with the words of Herschel Hobbs who said, "To violate man's free will would make him less than a person, only a puppet dangled on the string of fate. The Bible never teaches that. Man is free to choose, but is responsible to God for his choices. Otherwise, God Himself is responsible for man's sin. This is unthinkable!"[38]

THE ISSUE OF GOD'S PLAN AND HIS PEOPLE

As we have seen, the God we serve is a God of love, compassion, and mercy. He is also a God who takes sin seriously! It is because of our sinful-

Foreknowledge does not imply control!

ness and our inability to save ourselves that God sent forth His Son to offer the gift of eternal life, forgiveness for sin and the promise of an abundant life. It is also because of His desire that our love for Him would be a love of choice, not of coercion, that He gave free will to each one of us. How then can we interpret passages which do seem to indicate some kind of predestined call? Words such as predestined, election, etc., will be discussed in the next chapter. However, let it be said that all these words are biblical words and tell of the great truths of God's ministry toward us. Simply put, the Bible teaches that God elected a plan of salvation (Ephesians 1-2). He predestined that all who receive Jesus Christ would be a part of His elect family. He knew in advance exactly who would make that decision and who would not. Please know that just because He knew in advance did not mean that He controlled the outcome of the decision. Foreknowledge does not imply control! Again, an acceptance of such belief leads to a perversion of the true picture of God. Such a belief would make our wonderful, perfect heavenly Father responsible for sin.

God's plan through the ages is that He would provide a way for the salvation of humanity. Someone wisely said that the Bible is separated into two parts. First, there is Genesis 1-2 in which we see God's perfect plan expressed in the Garden of Eden. Then there is Genesis 3 through Revelation 22 where we see the second part of the Bible in which God does a wonderful work of redeeming sinful humanity; those who would allow such redemption. It was His plan to predestine the way of redemption. In other words, He did indeed predestine the *how* of redemp-

He did indeed predestine the how of redemption, not the who!

tion, not the *who!* To believe otherwise would be to deny God's gift of individual conscience, decision making power, and free will.

Not only did God elect a plan to determine the how of redemption, but He also chose a plan to propagate that way of redemption. In Ephesians 3:10-11, Paul wrote "that now, through the church, the manifold wisdom of God should be made known to the rulers and authorities in the heavenly realms, according to his eternal purpose which he accomplished in Christ Jesus our Lord." You may ask the question, "Why did God keep His secret about the church hidden for so many centuries?" Certainly the Old Testament clearly states that God will save the Gentiles through Israel, but nowhere are we told that both Jews and Gentiles will form a new creation, the church, the body of Christ. It was this mystery that the Spirit revealed to Paul and the other leaders in the early church, and that was so difficult for the Jews to accept. Paul tells us that the "rulers and authorities" are also involved in this great secret. God is educating the angels by means of the church! By the "rulers and authorities in the heavenly realms," Paul means the angelic beings created by God, both good and evil. Angels are created beings and are not omniscient. In fact, Peter indicates that during the Old Testament period, the angels were curious about God's plan of salvation then being worked out on earth (I Peter 1:10-12).

What then do the angels learn from the church? They learn "manifold wisdom of God." Certainly the angels know about the power of God as seen in His creation. The wisdom of God as seen in His new creation, the church, is something new to them. Unsaved mankind, including wise philosophers, look at God's plan of salvation and consider it foolishness (I Corinthians 1:18-31). But the angels watch the outworking of God's salvation, and they praise His wisdom. Paul calls it manifold wisdom, and this word carries the idea of "many-colored." This suggests the beauty and variety of God's wisdom in His great plan of salvation. But there is another facet to this truth that must be explored. What are the evil angels learning from God's mystery? They are learning that their leader, Satan, does not have any wisdom! Satan knows the Bible, and he understood from the Old Testament scriptures that the Savior would come, when He would come, how He would come, and where He would come. Satan also understood why He would come, as far as redemption is concerned. But nowhere in the Old Testament would Satan find any prophecies concerning the church, "the mystery" of Jews and Gentiles united in one body! Satan could see unbelieving Jews rejecting their Messiah, and he could see Gentiles trusting the Messiah. He could not see both believing Jews and Gentiles united in one body, seated with Christ in the heavenlies, and completely victorious over Satan! Had Satan known the far-reaching results of the cross, no doubt he would have altered his plans accordingly.

As you can see, God's wisdom is awesome! He has chosen a plan of redemption in which He has predestined the how of salvation. He has also chosen a people to propagate the plan of redemption and to spread that good news across the entire world. First Peter 2:1-10 clearly identifies the church as God's chosen people and that, "Once you were not a people, but you now are the people of God." God's people can reject either the way, the how of salvation, or they can reject God's plan to propagate that way. People are still responsible for the decisions they make to accept and follow or to reject!

THE INTERSECTION OF GOD'S SOVEREIGNTY AND MANKIND'S FREE WILL

There is much discussion in evangelical circles as to exactly how God's sovereign act of salvation intersects with a human being's response. As we have seen, some believe that salvation is an act initiated, carried out, and completed by the Lord only. On the other hand, others believe that the issue of free will and a human being's acceptance is of paramount importance. Even in the latter of those two groups, there is discussion as to actually how redemption occurs. There is a small, very vocal group of people who believe that faith alone (not repentance) is the avenue of free will acceptance. Others believe that the aspect of repentance and surrender must also accompany a person's free will acceptance. This brings forth many questions. Does mentioning repentance promote a "works" gospel? Does speaking of surrender in the process of salvation detract from the sovereign work of the Lord in salvation and redemption? As we attempt to answer these questions, let us remember some basic principles.

Salvation is the Act of a Sovereign God

This fact should alleviate much fear as we recognize that He is able to move in spite of our lack of agreement on specific terminology. Regeneration is a work of God's grace whereby believers become new creatures in Christ Jesus. It is a change of heart that is begun by the Holy Spirit through the conviction of sin. This change of heart which does include repentance, surrender, as well as faith is part of the Holy Spirit's drawing and convicting power. While a person must submit his or her will to God's drawing power, the power for any change or redemption comes only from the Lord.

Herschel Hobbs said it well, "Regeneration is the experience of being born again from above (John 3:3; Titus 3:5). It is an instantaneous work of God's grace wrought by the Holy Spirit through faith in Jesus Christ. Note that to create is a work of God, not of man (Ephesians 2:10)."[39]

There is the Limitation of Using Human Language to Describe a Divine Event

This principle must be understood. The weakness of every witnessing plan can be directly traced to this truth. Any human tool which attempts the description of a miraculous, God-produced event is bound to have limitations. All gospel explanations describe the act of salvation by delineating the requirements for salvation. The language that is used varies greatly. It is imperative that we recognize our limitations and express our honesty. Perhaps one of the greatest expressions of honesty while biblically accurate is the personal statement given by Howard Ramsey in his paper "As I Understand the Salvation Experience." When he said of the salvation experience, "When I became willing to turn to Him by faith, I simply committed all I knew of me to all I understood and knew of Him."[40]

The Bible is Not a Systematic Theology Textbook

In the Word of God, one finds an amazing variety of expressions used to describe the supernatural event of salvation. Boyd Hunt once said, "There are verbs for which the believer is the usual subject of the action described, such as repent and believe. These, and the endless related expressions, such as worship, obey, follow, endure, etc. are words appropriately describing what the believer does."[41]

For your information, the word "believe" is used 197 times in the New Testament (NIV version). The word "repent" is used in its various forms 52 times in the New Testament (NIV version). The word "save" is used in its various forms 89 times in the New Testament (NIV version). The phrase "born again" occurs three times in the New Testament (NIV Version). The word "salvation" is used 40 times in the New Testament (NIV version). The word "faith" is used 229 times in the New Testament (NIV

version). These facts help to show the validity of this principle. There are many ways to describe the wonderful
event of salvation.

It is not enough just to recognize the large number of
Scriptures which relate to salvation. Nor is it enough just
to recognize that the Scripture uses various terms to
describe the event of salvation. At this point, let us review
some of the specific biblical expressions which relate to
salvation and its various components.

• **Repentance**

The actual word "repentance" that is used in the
English language comes from a Latin derivation. It literally means to turn away (pento = turn; re = away or from).
The word that is used in the New Testament is the Greek
word "metanoeo" and literally means to perceive after-
wards (meta = after, implying change; noeo = to perceive).
It signifies a change in one's mind or purpose and in the
New Testament always implies a change for the better.[42] A
proper understanding of what repentance truly means
shows that it is a part of a genuine conversion experience.
While it is true that a person cannot repent of his/her own
accord, the obvious point is that for a person to be truly
saved, there must be a willingness to turn from that which
is improper and be willing to turn toward the God who
gives help. J. I. Packer states, "It is not enough to believe
that only through Christ and His death are sinners justified and accepted, and that one's own record is sufficient
to bring down God's condemning sentence twenty times
over and that, apart from Christ one has no hope.
Knowledge of the gospel and orthodox belief of it is no

substitute for repentance."[43] Billy Graham agrees when he says, "Thus, repentance is first, and absolutely necessary, if we are to be born again. It involves simple recognition of what we are but for God--sinners who fall short of His glory; second, it involves genuine sorrow for sin; third, it means our willingness to turn from sin."[44]

Following are just a few Scriptures in which repentance is shown to be absolutely imperative. A few of those are Matthew 3:8, Mark 1:15, Luke 3:8, 13:5, Acts 2:38, 3:19, 20:21, II Corinthians 7:10 and Hebrews 6:1.

• Faith

The word that is most often used for faith in the New Testament is the word "pistis" and literally means firm persuasion, trust, and conviction. J. I. Packer said it well, "Faith is essentially the casting and resting of oneself and one's confidence on the promises of mercy which Christ has given to sinners, and on the Christ who gave those promises . . . mere credence without trusting, and mere remorse without turning, do not save."[45] Faith is first of all belief. It does involve the knowledge of what God has done. It goes far beyond mere belief to an absolute trust. Remember the words of *The Baptist Faith and Message,* "Faith is the acceptance of Jesus Christ and commitment of the entire personality to Him as Lord and Savior." Please remember that faith does not save; grace saves. Faith, however, is the miraculous avenue through which we receive God's grace (Ephesians 2:8-9).

Following are several Scriptures which help us to recognize the importance of faith in receiving Jesus Christ.

Some of them are Mark 1:15, John 11:25-26, Acts 26:18, Romans 3:22, 4:5, 5:1, 10:9, Galatians 2:20, 3:24 and Hebrews 10:22.

• Lordship

In the New Testament, the word "Lord" comes from the Greek word "kurios" which is more properly an adjective, though is most often used as a noun. It literally refers to one who is an owner, master, or simply one to whom service is due. It is frequently used, as evidenced by the fact that in the New Testament it is found 576 times. To define the act of salvation by including the aspect of lordship is to recognize the clear teachings of the New Testament. Many have recognized this through the years. For example, the evangelist Billy Graham said, "What does it mean to believe? It means to 'commit' yourself to Christ, to 'surrender' to Him. Believing is your response to God's offer of mercy, love, and forgiveness."[46] Listen to the words of Boyd Hunt. "Since the believer's response is primarily a personal relationship between the believer and God, it involves the believer's whole person, from the beginning to the end of his Christian experience. The believer turns to God; he opens himself to what God wants to do for him in Christ. This is what it means to be a Christian, to expose oneself continuously to Christ as the shaper and determiner of one's style of life."[47]

Many of the faith-only adherents claim that the mention of lordship in the salvation experience is improper because of the inability of anyone to truly allow Jesus to be Lord in every aspect of life to the fullest degree. To make such an assertion is to have a total misunderstanding of what lordship and salvation means. To be saved does not require a life of lordship. It requires a heart which wishes to submit to Jesus as Lord and master. Obviously, the response of a believer in faith and repentance, and lordship will lead a person to a life of commitment to Christ. "The response is never final or perfect in this life. It remains always under the judgement of the biblical ideal. No one is ever fully the believer he ought to be."[48]

As mentioned earlier, the Scripture is literally full of examples which call for absolute commitment, or lordship when one receives Christ. Several of the most poignant examples are Matthew 16:24, Luke 9:23, 14:26, 14:33, Romans 10:9, Colossians 2:6-7 and James 2:18.

• Other Descriptions

The Scripture contains many expressions or descriptions of the salvation event. This confirms the principles stated earlier. Each biblical description, however, does provide additional light for us. It is obvious that an overall view of the Scripture shows forth a description of salvation that contains each of the above elements.

Examples of other New Testament expressions include Matthew 10:22, John 3:3, Acts 2:21 and Ephesians 1:5.

THE SCRIPTURAL DEFINITION OF KEY WORDS

PREDESTINATION

There are many Bible words which, when mentioned, immediately invoke an amazing array of thoughts, even emotions. The word "predestination" is certainly one of them! It is a word which has come to be charged with feelings of defensiveness, devotion, and for some, bewilderment. Let it be said that the doctrine of predestination is a precious doctrine which is set forth in the Word of God. It is a teaching which has been woefully misunderstood by some and neglected by most. It is quite obvious from the remainder of this book that I reject most of five point Calvinism. However, I do not reject the doctrine of predestination! I have tried to point out that there are many good men and women who have said many wrong things about the Lord. This is undoubtedly true in the area of predestination. There are some who sadly and mistakenly have stated that God predestines some to hell while He predestines others to heaven. Please know that God never predestined a person to hell and desires to save every person.

Can these verses be any clearer?

> The Lord is not slow in keeping his promise, as some understand slowness. He is patient with you, not wanting anyone to perish, but everyone to come to repentance. (II Peter 3:9)

> This is good, and pleases God our Savior, who wants all men to be saved and to come to a knowledge of the truth. (I Timothy 2:3-4)

> This is a trustworthy saying that deserves full acceptance (and for this we labor and strive), that we have put our hope in the living God, who is the Savior of all men, and especially of those who believe. (I Timothy 4:9-10)

Many people ask me, "How can anyone say that God has predestined some to hell, and some to heaven?" Many who believe such a misguided doctrine point to Romans 8:28-30 for proof.

> And we know that in all things God works for the good of those who love him, who have been called according to his purpose. For those God foreknew He also predestined to be conformed to the likeness of his Son, that he might be the first-born among many brothers. And those he predestined, he also called; those he called, he also justified; those he justified, he also glorified.

Again, let it be said that these verses present the truth of God's Word. They must not be avoided and certainly must not be misunderstood.

The Definition

Predestination is a divine act of the Lord whereby He makes redemption or adoption certain for the believer. Ephesians 1:5 says that God has "predestined us to be adopted as His sons through Jesus Christ, in accordance with His pleasure and will."

Remember that predestination deals with the certain accomplishment of one's adoption or redemption. When you are saved, you are made a son or daughter of God the moment of your salvation. However, even though you belong to the Lord Jesus now,

Predestination is a divine act of the Lord whereby He makes redemption or adoption certain for the believer.

you have not arrived at the goal which God has predestined you to, which is adoption or final redemption. This is what Paul is talking about in Ephesians 1:5. This ultimate redemption does not occur at the moment of salvation, but at the resurrection of our bodies. This is clearly stated in Romans 8:23 when it says, "Not only so, but we ourselves, who have the first fruits of the Spirit, groan inwardly as we wait eagerly for our adoption as sons, the redemption of our bodies." Yes, it is true that our souls are redeemed at the moment of salvation, but our ultimate redemption and adoption will take place when we have redeemed souls in redeemed bodies. Our adoption or final redemption is certain since it was predestined that every believer shall arrive at that goal! Yes, I believe in predestination! The scripture is clear that the ultimate redemption and therefore adoption of human beings is made certain by the Lord. Until that occurs, we have been given the wonderful "spirit of adoption" which is referred to in Romans 8:15.

Who is to Be Redeemed?

Predestination is God making certain of the ultimate redemption of His children. According to Galatians 4:5,

Jesus Christ came to redeem all those who were under the law. Who was under the law? Would not any serious Bible student agree that everyone was under the demand of the law as well as under the penalty of the law? The scripture says that Jesus Christ came that we might receive the adoption of sons. God's desire is that this be accomplished for all. As we have already seen, the reality is that all will not receive this gift. This does not negate God's purpose, nor His heart-felt desire.

To know that He has accomplished on the cross the greatest gift ever imagined is an awesome thought. To be ultimately redeemed, and adopted finally and fully into God's family is a tremendous privilege. We ought to pause and give thanks to the Lord for His wonderful gift, enabled by the shed blood of Jesus Christ!

What is the Purpose of Predestination?

The purpose is that we ultimately be redeemed. Look again to Romans 8:28-30. In v. 29, the purpose of predestination is stated very clearly. It is that we might be conformed to the image of His Son. In other words, to be adopted or fully redeemed is to be totally like the Lord Jesus. Predestination is the guarantee, the pledge of certainty that this will occur.

Though the word predestine or predestined is used only four times in the King James Version as well as in the New International Version, it is a precious doctrine. Another part of the purpose of predestination deals with the church. The work of the Spirit of God is to bring members into the body of Christ. In the book of Ephesians, Paul is dealing with the body of Christ. I believe that most scholars would agree that Paul is not speaking of individual believers in this book so much as he is speaking of the church as a whole. Ephesians 1:4 tells that before the foundation of the world, God decided He would have a church. He decided that the church would have its foundation "in Him."[49]

Herschel Hobbs is right when he says, "Unfortunately many tend to interpret the English word predestination rather than the Greek word proorisas." As he says, the basic verb is horizo, which means among other things to set a boundary. From it comes our English word "horizon," which is the limit or boundary of your vision from where you stand. The prefix pro means beforehand. So it means to set a boundary beforehand. Hobbs likens it to building a fence around a piece of land. "The fence is Christ." In eleven verses (1:3-13) Paul uses "in Christ" and its equivalent eleven times (in the Greek text).[50]

The Lord not only decided to have a church which He would have united with Christ, but he decided what kind of church that would be, and He decided it before the foundation of the world. He wanted it to be a church that would be without blame. He wanted a church that would be perfect and without fault. He determined that He would make certain that the church would be ultimately redeemed. That is exactly what is talked about in Ephesians 1:4-5. God never predestined an individual to heaven or an individual to hell. Christ did decide the destination of the church and that is the truth of predestination's purpose. People who are predestined are those who belong to the body of Christ. You are predestined the moment you are saved, because at that moment you become a member of the body of Christ. Please remember He predestined the how, not the who!

Remember that justification by faith in Jesus is the way that leads to predestination. The moment that God saves a human being, the Spirit of God places him or her in the body of Christ, and as soon as that person is in the body of Christ, he or she is in the divinely predestined body of Christ. John 1:12 states it clearly, "Yet to all who received him, to those who believed in his name, he gave the right to become children of God."

The moment that God saves a human being, the Spirit of God places him or her in the body of Christ, and as soon as that person is in the body of Christ, he or she is in the divinely predestined body of Christ.

ELECTION

The doctrine of election is another area of misunderstanding, confusion, and sometimes misapplication. It is a word like predestination that brings forth strong emotions. Though it is used a few more times than the word predestination, it does speak of a great purpose from the heart of our Lord. It is because the scriptures wish for us to know the truth about God's plan, we must ponder what God's Word says about this great Bible doctrine. Perhaps one of the most often used scriptures, in regards to election is Romans 9. We will look at several verses from this great chapter as we study the doctrine of election.

Let us remember the definitions which we have already used. Predestination is the divine act whereby God makes certain the goal of adoption or final redemption for the believer. Ephesians 1:5 shows that this is God's ultimate purpose for His children. It is His wish

> *Election is a descriptive term and is used to refer to rank and privilege, not deliverance from damnation or eternal torment.*

that those who have accepted Him become a part of God's family and therefore also a part of God's elect. The Bible does speak about the elect of God or God's elect. It is important to note that when the phrase is used it is not a mere statement of fact or even of purpose, but like the scriptural expression "first born," it is a title of dignity and that title is only applied to those who are believers. It is a descriptive term and is used to refer to rank and privilege, not deliverance from damnation or eternal torment.

The Definition of Election

As we have been reminded of the definition of predestination, let us come to a clearly discernable understanding of the word election. Election is a divine act of God, whereby God sets aside all firsts and chooses all seconds to achieve the accomplishment of His plan. Hebrews 10:9 says, "Then he said, 'Here I am, I have come to do your will.' He sets aside the first to establish the second." Election is a divine act of God, a sovereign God, whereby God sets to one side all firsts and chooses all seconds to accomplish His purpose. There were many offerings and sacrifices in the Old Testament and they were called the firsts because they were in the Jewish plan of God's purpose. God set them to one side at the beginning of the age of grace in which we now live. It was the will of God to set the "first plan" aside and choose for the blessing of mankind the sacrifice and offering of Christ.

The outstanding picture of the principles of election is seen in Genesis 48:2-20. Notice carefully that Israel blessed Joseph's two sons Ephraim and Manasseh. However remember that Ephraim was the younger and Manasseh was the older. In order for the father to put his right hand on Ephraim who was the younger, he had to cross his hands or arms. Much to the consternation of Joseph, God led Israel to choose the second over the first.

This principle was stated often and in many ways by our Lord Jesus. For example in Luke 9:48 He said, "For he who is least among you all–he is the greatest." In Mark 9:35 He said, "If anyone wants to be first, he must be the very last, and the servant of all."

It is obvious that our Lord often chose to use what would seem to the world a second choice. In God's sovereign purpose, He has often chosen the less to lead the greater, the weak to rule the stronger. God's election is His sovereign wisdom at work. He has chosen, for example, Israel who was considered the smallest of all peoples to be a light unto the world. God chose in the ministry of His Son Jesus to use disciples who definitely would not have been the world's first choice. Election is a divine act of God whereby God uses the second and sets aside the first to accomplish His divinely ordained purposes.

What is the Purpose of Election?

Perhaps one of the most often used (or abused) passages in regards to election is Romans 9. Please note that election is *not* God choosing or electing some to be saved and some to be lost. In fact to say so is charging God with doing something that He cannot do, because He has provided salvation for every human being who would receive and accept it. To say that God has chosen or elected some to be lost would limit the atonement of Jesus Christ. Remember that this is one of the duties of Satan. It is always his intent to limit the work of Christ on the cross. For God to elect some to salvation and others to damnation is to label God as a respecter of persons, and that leads one to believe that the Holy Spirit only deals with certain people, and that is those who are chosen or elected. If that is true, Christ's death was not for all mankind. The scripture says otherwise!

Some people believe that Romans 9:11 teaches that God chooses some for eternal life and others for eternal damnation. "Yet, before the twins were born or had done anything good or bad–in order that God's purpose in election might stand."

This passage does not teach that God has elected some to heaven and some to hell. On the contrary, this verse tells us about the purpose of God according to election. Now notice Romans 9:12, "Not by works but by him who calls–she was told, 'The older will serve the younger.'" The purpose of election is that the elder will serve the younger.

Remember our previous discussion in which we have shown that God often chose the younger to lead the older.

Election is God's way of selecting His servants to do His bidding. The issue is service, not salvation.

The greater often serves the lesser. Again, it is God setting to one side the first and choosing the second. Election is God's way of selecting His servants to do His bidding. The issue is service, not salvation.

What are the Most Often Misunderstood Passages Regarding Election?

Does Romans 9:15-18 teach some are elected to salvation and some to damnation? Some believe that this teaches that if an unconverted person dies in their sins, it is because God did not have mercy on them, thus they were of the non-predestined or non-elect. That is not the teaching of this verse. Please remember that all the truth concerning God's mercy and heart toward unsaved people is not found in just one verse. Romans 9:18 is not the entirety of the scripture, but on the other hand it certainly does *not* teach us everything about the mercy of God.

What does this verse teach? To truly understand about God's mercy, look further to Romans 11:32 to see how God's mercy is manifest. It is obvious that God wished to have mercy on everyone! The issue which is portrayed in Romans 9:17-18 is the issue of God dealing with the hard hearts of those such as Pharaoh so that God's glory would be manifest and His power brought to light. I believe that those who purposefully hardened themselves against God have placed themselves in a situation where they were used to portray the awesome power and plan of God. Those who are already hardening their hearts (Exodus 7:22ff) placed themselves in a position so that God could use them to display His power. Yes, it is true from the Exodus account as well as the Romans account that God continued to harden their hearts so that His plan might be manifest. While you may have difficulty with such teaching, please see that it has nothing to do with the selection of some to damnation, but simply of God's election for the manifestation of His plan and purpose.

Some look to Romans 9:22-23 to show that God has elected some for salvation and some for damnation. Please notice that v. 22 speaks about the vessels of wrath fitted to destruction. In the Greek text there is no pronoun "his." God never fitted any person for destruction! It is Satan who has fitted humans for destruction. God endured with great patience the vessels who yielded themselves to the devil. Note that Satan is the one who makes us vessels of wrath and prepares us for hell. God has done everything, including the sending of His Son to reverse that satanic purpose.

It is Satan who has fitted humans for destruction.

Some feel that Acts 13:48 is a passage which teaches God's appointing some to believe and some not to believe. Does this verse teach that some are appointed to be saved and others not? Please notice the context of this verse. It teaches that Barnabas and Paul had been preaching the gospel to the Jews. The Jews refused to respond to their ministry. These two servants of the Lord turned from ministering to the Jews for the time being and turned their faces toward the Gentile population. The context of this passage shows that God is turning the ministry of these men to the Gentiles. This was in God's plan. He wanted the Gentiles to hear the good news. This text does not teach that God had planned to save just a few of those Gentiles on that occasion. While offering salvation to all Gentiles, some of the Gentiles believed that day what the Jews had rejected. Those Gentiles who were willing to receive salvation and whose minds were open to the truth were ready to believe. This group happened to be a few of the Gentiles who were present and believed and were saved.

One of the most often used verses to portray a false view of election is Romans 9:13. Please realize that God did not say this before Jacob and Esau were born. This statement was recorded in the last book of the Old Testament, Malachi 1:2-3(long after their birth). Notice the phrase in Romans 9:13, "as it is written." It is recorded as being written back in the book of Malachi. What was recorded? God's hatred toward Esau and his descendants is the subject of that writing. Why would God "hate" Esau and his descendants? It was because of their continued wickedness and idolatry. This does not refer to individual persons (Jacob and Esau), but to the nations they represent. God was better able to use Jacob's line to carry out His wishes.

Some question Matthew 22:14ff in regards to the subject of election. When the scripture in this passage refers to the fact that "many are called, but few are chosen," is this not referring to some kind of election? In essence, it is saying that many people hear the summons of the gospel, but only a certain percentage respond properly. As pointed out earlier, Jesus predicted this in the Sermon on the Mount. However, this is interesting use of election terminology. "Kletoi" (literally, called) is not to be taken here as irresistible calling but in the sense of "invited." Those responding properly may well be said to have been chosen or elected. The called are the true community of the people God chooses to save, even as Israel had once been so chosen. But those individuals must freely respond to the Holy Spirit's convicting and drawing power in their lives. The imagery here is in fact more that of corporate than of individual selection.

Who are the People Who are Elected?

Nowhere in the Bible is election connected with the salvation or the damnation of human beings. Who are the elect? They are the saved people, His favored ones. Israel in the Old Testament is God's elect. Isaiah 45:3-4 teaches this truth. In the New Testament, we see that the church is His body, God's elect. First Peter 2:4-5 teaches this unmistakable truth. This rank or privilege is shown to those people not before they are saved, but only after.

FOREKNOWLEDGE

We have been studying words which are often used in regards to the subject in question. We have looked at words such as predestination, adoption, and election. Whereas these are acts of God, foreknowledge is not a divine act as much as it is a divine attribute.

The Definition of Foreknowledge

Foreknowledge is a divine attribute of God, whereby God sees all things and knows all things in the present tense. In other words, there is no past, present, or future with God. Second Peter 3:8 says, "With the Lord a day is like a thousand years, and a thousand years are like a day." It is important to note that with God, neither time nor space limits Him in any way. It is important to note this if we are going to understand foreknowledge.

A Clarification of Its Extent

Somehow, those who have gone to an extreme belief in Calvinism have adopted a belief that because God knows what will take place, therefore He is totally responsible for all that does take place. Calvinism prides itself on being a logical system. Some believe that the logic of Calvinism pulls them to the conclusion that since God has predestined salvation, His control extends far beyond that aspect of life. Please keep in mind the definition–that foreknowledge is a divine attribute, not an act. It is a serious misinterpretation of the scripture and a misapplication of understanding God's true nature to believe that because God knows everything ahead of time, He can be blamed with the act of determining all the deeds of mankind. The fact of God's foreknowledge admits that He

The fact of God's foreknowledge admits that He is certain of all that will take place, but His foreknowledge does not determine what will take place.

is certain of all that will take place, but His foreknowledge does not determine what will take place. In other words, foreknowledge does not imply control! To believe this would make God the author of sin. That simply is not true!

There are those in many fields of science who have reached an amazing degree of predictive ability. Actuaries are persons who work for insurance companies and are experts at determining the probability of life span based on recorded statistics of previous occurrences. These highly paid professionals work diligently to make sure that the insurance company will take the right risk on the right person. Astronomers have become extremely adept at predicting eclipses and other astronomical phenomenon. Even with some glaring mistakes, meteorologists have become much better at predicting the occurrences of tor-nadoes, hurricanes, and other violent weather. Does the ability of any of these professionals to foreknow imply that any must therefore be able to control? The answer is obviously no! I think most would recognize that parents who have lived with children for years begin to know how to predict the behavior and temperament of children in certain situations and in certain ways. Again, does this foreknowledge imply control? Recognizing that human beings can only know in part, we recognize that the Lord knows in full. Foreknowledge does not imply or require control either on a human or divine level.

In the scriptural illustration in Romans 8, Paul pulls together all the beautiful words which we have been studying. In v. 29, he tells that he knows what is going to happen to those who are a part of the family of God. Notice how this connects with our study in predestina-tion. As stated earlier, predestination is God making certain the final redemption or adoption of believers. Again in Romans 8:29, this truth is powerfully represented. God knew who was going to be saved and as a part of that foreknowledge He also guarantees that those who have accepted Christ will become like His Son, Jesus Christ.

Notice the closing statement in Romans 8:30, "Those he justified, he also glorified." God speaks of all these transactions as though they had already taken place. Mankind is called, foreknown, justified, predestined, and glorified. All these are in the mind of God as if they were in the present tense. God sees our glorification as though it were present and complete. Now we know that it is not complete in experience, for we have not yet been glorified. However, because of His precious predestination, His future for us is present knowledge with God, and He sees the believer's glorification as though it were in the present before Him.[51]

God sees our glorification as though it were present and complete.

In Psalm 139:1-8, we see yet another scriptural use of the concept of foreknowledge. Here we have the testimony of King David concerning the foreknowledge of God. In the first verse, David declares that God knows Him. In the second verse he declares that God knows every thought that is being formed even before it is expressed in words. In v. 3, he declares that God knows the whole conduct of his life and in v. 5 he reminds himself that God knows him totally at all times and in all places. In v. 6, David points out that such knowledge is too wonderful. Here he is dealing with the subject of foreknowledge which is a divine attribute. God knows and understands our lives just as He understood and knew David's life, before it ever occurred.

To trust in the foreknowledge of God is to know that our God is an awesome, powerful God. To believe in the foreknowledge of God makes our prayer lives even more special as we ask God to help us, knowing that He knows what is best for us in the long term.

What an awesome God we have! He is the God of Abraham, Isaac, and Jacob. He is the God and Father of our Lord Jesus Christ. He knows the past, present, and the future. He is a God of love toward His children and wise in His planning for them. God knows everything about us, yet still loves us. The words of I Peter 3:12 are beautiful, "For the eyes of the Lord are on the righteous and His ears are attentive to His prayer, but the face of the Lord is against those who do evil." We ought to thank God for the salvation He has given us. Included in that salvation is the gift of spiritual fruit (Galatians 3:22-23), and spiritual gifts (I Corinthians 12:4-7, Romans 12:6-8), as well as powerful spiritual armor with which we can achieve victory (Ephesians 6:10-24).

God's foreknowledge brings joy and gladness to the believer's heart, for we know that God knows perfectly the road ahead, though we do not. Romans 11:33-36 says it well:

Oh, the depth of the riches of the wisdom and knowledge of God! How unsearchable his judgements, and his paths beyond tracing out! 'Who has known the mind of the Lord? Or who has been his counselor?' 'Who has ever given to God, that God should repay him?' For from him and through him and to him are all things. To him be the glory forever! Amen.

CONCLUSION

In recent days, there has been a resurgence of the promotion of the doctrine of Calvinism within evangelical circles. One positive result of this is that it has brought a renewed study of God's Word and its truths regarding salvation. The downside of this resurgence is that many people are falling into a trap set long ago. Manmade doctrines always fail. When any person or person begins to adhere to the teachings of one person, they join the company of many others who have made this serious mistake. It is most grievous to see a large number of individuals accept without question the doctrine of John Calvin in regards to salvation. This acceptance of his manmade system of logic has led many to say things about God which are simply unbelievable! For example, one writer says, "Even the works of Satan are so controlled and limited that they serve God's purposes. While Satan eagerly desires the destruction of the wicked and diligently works to bring it about, yet the destruction proceeds from God. It is in the first place, God who decrees that the wicked shall suffer and Satan is merely permitted to lay the punishment upon them."[52] Yet God's Word says in John 3:17, "For God did not send His Son into the world to condemn the world, but to save the world through Him." What a contrast! On the one hand we see a manmade system of logic and on the other hand we see the truth of God's Word.

William Estep is right when he says that, "This new-found fascination with Calvinism and the system of theology that bears his name is both intriguing and puzzling, since most of the ardent advocates of this movement have only a slight knowledge of Calvin or his system as set forth in the *Institutes of the Christian Religion.*" This world renowned historian is right in saying, "It is a system of theology without biblical support."[53] Manmade doctrines will always fail!

It is also important to remember that manmade doctrines always hurt God's work. Wynkoop is right in saying, "This fixed faith theology is reflected in a lack of evangelistic urgency. Either there is no evangelistic program at all (since to offer an invitation to men would constitute a defiance against God's sovereign will) or the preaching appeal is made with conviction that only the elect and all the elect will respond. Such preaching often lacks the gracious, heartbroken, tender, winsome appeal of the preacher who, as Paul, made every kind of personal sacrifice in order to commend himself as Christ's messenger to men in order to win them to his Lord."[54] She goes on to say that some high Calvinists have refused to cooperate with evangelist Billy Graham because he dares to invite men to Christ and this makes him therefore an Arminian.[55]

If one does follow the logic of Hyper-Calvinism, then a missionary or evangelistic spirit is unnecessary. If irresistible grace is the truth, then there is no urgent need to share Christ with anyone, since those persons whom God has elected are irresistibly going to be drawn into His kingdom anyway. If ones studies the pages of history, one will see that Calvinistic theology (Five Point) has encouraged a slackening of the aggressive evangelistic and missionary heartbeat of the church. All too often, this precious spirit of concern and urgency is replaced by a cold, logical, haughty spirit.

Roy Fish from Southwestern Baptist Theological Seminary accurately points out what happens when true Calvinism takes hold of a denomination. He says, "Calvinism has virtually brought to a standstill evangelism in certain Baptist groups. They believe that if God was going to save people that He would not do it through human instrumentalities. Like Rylands said to missionary William Carey, 'If He wants to convert somebody, He will do it without you or me.'" This particular group called the Primitive Baptists or Hard-shell Baptists are one of several groups who have almost gone out of existence because they rejected evangelism and the winning of people to Jesus Christ through sharing the message with them.[56]

Manmade doctrines must always give way to God's Word! When one begins to become aware of the slide of persons away from God's Word to an adherence to manmade doctrine, those who have a heart of belief for the infallible Word of God must proclaim that truth. Those who hold to an adherence of devotion to God's Word must proclaim its superiority to manmade doctrine. In other words, let the scripture speak for itself! For example, what could be clearer than I Timothy 4:10 which says, "And for this we labor and strive, that we have put our hope in the living God, who is the Savior of all men, and especially of those who believe"? Hyper-Calvinists have a problem with this verse because the expression "all men" *must* here be understood as referring to all mankind. The verse teaches that God's salvation has indeed appeared to all but that the hope of a living God deals especially with those who believe. This text teaches the truth of all of God's Word–that God came to seek and save that which was lost. He loves all people, came to reach out to all people. Also, however, as this verse points out, only some believe.

In other words, let the scripture speak for itself!

Herschel Hobbs said it well when he described John 3:16. "For God so loved the world (not certain ones in it), that He gave His only begotten Son, that whosoever (anyone, anywhere, anytime) believeth (an act of man's free will) in Him should not perish (be lost, destroyed, or go to hell), but have everlasting life."[57] God's Word is clear. Let it speak for itself.

ENDNOTES

1. Curt Daniel, *Biblical Calvinism*, (Madison, Ala.: Kenton L. Haynes, 1994), p. 1.

2. R. B. Kuiper, *For Whom Did Christ Die?*, (Grand Rapids: William B. Eerdmans Publishing Co., 1959), p. 37.

3. Loraine Boettner, *The Reform Doctrine of Predestination*, 8th ed., (Grand Rapids: William B. Eerdmans Publishing Co., 1954), p. 59.

4. William Shed, *Dogmatic Theology*, (New York: Charles Scribner's Sons Publisher, 1888), 2:460.

5. Mildred Bangs Wynkoop, *Foundations of Wesleyan-Arminian Theology*, (Kansas City: Beacon Hill Press, 1967), p. 23.

6. Robert A. Baker, *A Summary of Christian History*, (Nashville: Broadman Press, 1959), p. 78.

7. Ibid., p. 79.

8. Wynkoop, Foundations, p. 37.

9. Ibid., p. 39.

10. John Calvin, *Institutes of the Christian Religion*, trans. Henry Beveridge, (Grand Rapids: William B. Eerdmans Publishing Co., 1957), 2:203.

11. Wynkoop, p. 98.

12. Iain H. Murray, *The Forgotten Spurgeon*, (London: The Banner of Truth Trust, 1966), p. 59.

13. Ibid., p. 62.

14. Ibid., p. 210.

15. Herschel Hobbs, *The Christian Index*, 11 May 1995.

16. Dwayne Edward Spencer, *TULIP*, (Grand Rapids: Baker Book House, 1979), p. 11.

17. W. J. Seaton, *The Five Points of Calvinism*, (London: The Banner of Truth Trust, 1970), p. 5.

18. Spencer, *TULIP*, p. 32.

19. Daniel, *Biblical Calvinism*, p. 1.

20. Calvin, *Institutes*, Book III, chapter 21A, quoted in Wynkoop, Foundations, p. 40.

21. Seaton, *Five Points*, p. 8.

22. Boettner, *Reform Doctrine*, p. 121.

23. Ibid., p. 97.

24. Ibid., p. 242.

25. Seaton, *Five Points*, p. 9.

26. Spencer, *TULIP*, p. 40.

27. Daniel, *Biblical Calvinism*, p. 6.

28. Kuiper, *For Whom*, p. 27.

29. Shed, *Dogmatic Theology*, p. 464.

30. Seaton, *Five Points*, p. 14.

31. Boettner, *Reform Doctrine*, p. 214.

32. Hobbs, *Christian Index*.

33. Wynkoop, *Foundations*, p. 98.

34. W. T. Conner quoted in Darrell W. Robinson, *The Doctrine of Salvation*, (Nashville: Convention Press, 1992), p. 25.

35. Roy Fish, sermon preached at Cottage Hill Baptist Church, Mobile, Alabama, August 11, 1997.

36. Boettner, *Reform Doctrine*, p. 101.

37. Ibid., p. 118.

38. Hobbs, *Christian Index.*

39. Herschel Hobbs, *The Baptist Faith and Message*, (Nashville: Convention Press, 1971), p. 60.

40. Howard Ramsey, "As I Understand the Salvation Experience."

41. Boyd Hunt "Toward a Doctrine of the Christian Life," *Southwestern Journal of Theology*, Spring 1978, p. 21.

42. W. E. Vine, *An Expository Dictionary of New Testament Words*, (Lynchburg, Virginia: The Old-Time Gospel Hour), p. 952.

43. J. I. Packer, *Evangelism and the Sovereignty of God*, (Dowers Grove, Illinois: InterVarsity Press, 1961), pp. 71-72.

44. Billy Graham, *How to Be Born Again*, (Carmel, New York: Guideposts, 1977), p. 160.

45. *Evangelism and the Sovereignty of God*, pp. 70-71.

46. *How to Be Born Again*, p. 161.

47. *Southwestern Journal of Theology*, Spring 1978, p. 26.

48. *Southwestern Journal of Theology*, Spring 1978, p. 26.

49. Andrew Telford, *Subjects of Sovereignty*, (Philadelphia: The Berachah Church), p. 35.

50. Hobbs, *The Christian Index.*

51. Telford, *Subjects of Sovereignty*, p. 66-67.

52. Boettner, *Reform Doctrine*, p. 243.

53. William R. Estep, *Baptist Standard*, March 19, 1997.

54. Wynkoop, Foundations, p. 63.

55. Ibid., p. 63.

56. Roy Fish, Cottage Hill Baptist Church.

57. Hobbs, *The Christian Index.*